A Concise History of a Hundred Years of Papal Teaching on Catholic Education

Rev. Nicholas L. Gregoris, STD, EdD

En Route Books and Media, LLC
Saint Louis, MO

En Route Books and Media, LLC
5705 Rhodes Avenue
St. Louis, MO 63109

Contact us at **contactus@enroutebooksandmedia.com**

Cover Credit: Sebastian Mahfood

Copyright 2024 Nicholas L. Gregoris

ISBN-13: 979-8-88870-157-7
Library of Congress Control Number: 2024935604

All rights reserved. No part of this book may be reproduced, stored in a retrieval system, or transmitted in any form, or by any means, electronic, mechanical, photocopying, or otherwise, without the prior written permission of the author.

Table of Contents

Foreword iii

Introduction 1

Benedict XV 7

Pius XI 9

Venerable Pius XII 15

Saint John XXIII 29

Saint Paul VI 35

Blessed John Paul I 43

Saint John Paul II 51

Benedict XVI 69

Francis 81

Conclusion 87

Foreword

Education is essentially a human enterprise, and, as Pope Benedict XVI recalled, the Church is "an expert in humanity." Pope John XXIII entitled one of his encyclicals *Mater et Magistra* (Mother and Teacher); indeed, because the Church is a loving Mother, she is a reliable and dedicated Teacher. She has exercised that role in a pre-eminent fashion through the Catholic school which, as Pope John Paul II was fond of saying, is the very "heart of the Church."

The Mission of Catholic Schools: A Century of Ecclesial Reflection and Direction (co-published by the National Catholic Educational Association and Newman House Press; see the notice at the end of this volume) originated from the repeated wish of "practitioners" to have a handy collection of ecclesiastical documents on Catholic schools. Under that rubric were included papal teachings, as well as texts from the Second Vatican Council, the Congregation for Catholic Education, the *Code of Canon Law*, the *Catechism of the Catholic Church*, and the *Compendium of the Social Doctrine of the Church*. Although the Church has been engaged in the education apostolate from her earliest days, it was deemed necessary to take on a reasonable focus – a century of reflection seemed to fit the bill, beginning with the pontificate of Benedict XV and ending with that of Francis.

Given that both Father Nicholas Gregoris and I are the products of a total Catholic education and have taught in Catholic schools at every level – elementary, secondary, university and seminary – we called on that experience to assist in the selection process. We trust our judgment has proven valid. Most of the material up to the pontificate of Pope John Paul II required translation from Latin, Italian, French, or Spanish – which task Father Gregoris assumed with great gusto and expertise. His indispensable work on that project was deemed worthy of earning his doctorate in Catholic school administration from Pontifex University, the text of which defense it is a pleasure to offer to the present readers.

Who will benefit from this anthology? Bishops and priests, parents, teachers and administrators, school and finance boards, potential donors, religious superiors, and public policy promoters. The

Foreword

material provided will be useful in curriculum development, Catholic identity assessment, faculty professional seminars and days of recollection, as well as in the production of mission statements and in the creation of promotional pieces.

Most people connect Saint John Henry Cardinal Newman to university education, failing to realize that the real "apple of his eye" was his Oratory School. So strong was Saint John Henry's advocacy on behalf of Catholic schools that in 1879 the Archbishop of Sydney, Roger Bede Vaughan, solicited his assistance for the cause in Australia. To which, the newly minted Cardinal replied:

> . . . I feel it a great honour on the part of Your Grace, that you have made use, in the Pastorals, which you have had the goodness to send me, of what I had occasion to say at Rome last May on the subject of the special religious evil of the day. It pleased me to find that you could make it serviceable in the anxious conflict in which you are at this time engaged in defence of Christian education. It is indeed the gravest of questions whether our people are to commence life with

or without adequate instruction in those all-important truths which ought to colour all thought and to direct all action; – whether they are or are not to accept this visible world for their God and their all, its teaching as their only truth, and its prizes as their highest aims; – for, if they do not gain, when young, that sacred knowledge which comes to us from Revelation, when will they acquire it?

". . . *if they do not gain, when young, that sacred knowledge which comes to us from Revelation, when will they acquire it?*" It was the very same conviction that moved us to undertake this project. In many ways, it was a labor of love and an act of gratitude for our own faith and vocation which were nurtured in the Church's schools. We pray that the Church's perennial wisdom in the educational sphere, memorialized in our anthology, will continue to nourish the faith of generations to come.

Reverend Peter M. J. Stravinskas, Ph.D., S.T.D.
President, Catholic Education Foundation
Dean, Faculty of Education, Pontifex University

Introduction

Dear Provost Clayton, Rev. and Dear Fathers Stravinskas and Davis, Dr. Sebastian Mahfood, OP, *Salutem in Domino et Laudetur Jesus Christus*!

I must admit that doing a second doctorate at the ripe old age of 50 has left me feeling a bit like Rodney Dangerfield in that classic 80s comedy, "Back to School," or perhaps more like Michael Corleone, played by the aging Al Pacino in "Godfather III," when he cries out in anguish, "Just when I thought I was out, they pull me back in!"

Seriously, I am honored and privileged to be here today. I am most grateful to you for hosting me for this doctoral defense. In particular, I want to thank our Dean, Father Stravinskas, for his steadfast guidance of this entire process under the capable leadership of Provost Clayton.

Father Stravinskas first taught me to seek wisdom in Saint Augustine's little masterpiece, *De Magistro* ("On the Teacher"). He not only taught me Latin in high school but also my first college courses in Biblical Greek and Philosophy of Education. I learned from him the true meaning of the adages: *fides quærens intellectum*;[1] *contemplata aliis tradere*;[2] and *discimus docendo*.[3]

As a college seminarian, he inspired me: to attend a week-long immersion course in Latin; participate in a seminar on Catholic journalism; offer adult catechism classes at his parish; and teach conversational Latin at a nearby Catholic elementary school.

After ordination, he encouraged me to teach at a Catholic high school, join the faculty of the Pontifical College Josephinum, serve as the first full-time chaplain of Wyoming Catholic College, publish my doctoral dissertation with Newman House Press, partner with him as managing editor of *The Catholic Response*, and pursue this education degree. Most especially, Father Stravinskas has modeled for me what it means to love Christ's Sacred Priesthood and to cherish the unique role of the priest as educator both in and outside of the

---

[1] "Faith seeking understanding," attributed to Saint Anselm of Canterbury.

[2] "What you have contemplated hand on to others," a motto of the Order of Preachers.

[3] "We learn by teaching," a phrase dear to ancient Romans like Cicero.

classroom.

Therefore, with a spirit of gratitude, I would like to pray in the words of the late Monsignor Luigi Giussani, author of the renowned work, *Il Rischio Educativo* ("The Educational Risk") and Founder of the "Communion and Liberation" movement. Imbued with a devotion to Cardinal Newman and his seminal work entitled *Idea of a University*, he often prayed in these simple yet profound words: "*Veni, Sancte Spiritus, veni per Mariam!*" ("Come Holy Spirit, come through Mary"). This pithy prayer has served me well throughout the years, especially when tasked with teaching and preaching God's Word. I first learned it while studying at the Pontifical Lateran University, where I served as English translator for the former *Rector Magnificus*, Cardinal Angelo Scola.

Moreover, I am proud that, despite many a setback, my journey thus far has been the felicitous and fortuitous culmination of a lifetime of education in the heart of the Church from elementary school through graduate school. Without Catholic education, especially as I experienced it with so many consecrated men and women of different religious orders, I would not be the man, let alone the priest, that I am today!

With that basic background in place, and acknowledging that Newman was in fact himself "personalist to the core," I dedicate my defense today to the blessed memory of all my deceased teachers – mindful of the fact that the methodology and scope of this second doctorate are quite different from those they taught me to employ decades ago. Permit me to explain.

The present doctoral project was uniquely comprised of translating hundreds of pages of mainly Italian texts; some were also in Latin, Spanish, and French, which had hitherto never been translated into English. These texts belonged to a special category, namely, the magisterium of the Supreme Pontiffs of the past one hundred years ranging from Benedict XV to Francis. The topic, generally speaking, was Catholic education, and the themes ranged from the liberal arts and social sciences to theology, "the Queen of the Sciences," and philosophy, her "handmaiden." The bulk of my translation work dealt with the writings of Pius XII and John Paul II. The latter often composed in Polish and had his work translated into Italian by priests working in the Secretariat of State. This proved to be a source of great frustration for me since I neither speak Polish nor am I privy to the Polish mindset, while I am in fact fluent in Italian and very well-versed in Italian culture due to my heritage, upbringing and study abroad. On the other hand, the florid Italian expressions of Pius XII were about as familiar to me as the Victorian turns of phrase found on every page of Newman's corpus, which I was challenged to master to obtain my first doctorate.

As I translated these papal documents, I was frequently reminded of Saint John Paul II's saying that the Catholic school is the very "heart of the Church" and of his encyclical *Fides et Ratio* (1998), whose poetic opening lines are etched in stone at Walsh Library at my Alma Mater, Seton Hall University, the nation's oldest diocesan university, founded by Saint Elizabeth Ann Seton's nephew who, as Bishop of Newark, named it in her honor. John Paul II famously wrote, "Faith and reason are like two wings on which the human spirit rises to the contemplation of truth."

In this presentation, therefore, rather than get

bogged down in the minutiae of a complex 1,067-page anthology, which also includes ample sections on "Papal Documents," "Second Vatican Council," "Documents of the Holy See," "Saintly Teachers" and an "Appendix of Documents of the United States Conference of Catholic Bishops," I thought it would be more beneficial to look at the big picture – situating each of the last six popes in his own proper historical and theological context – in order to demonstrate the interconnectedness of their magisterial contributions with their particular reflections and directions on Catholic education as revealed in select texts of the anthology.

My initial translations were a bit daunting because I was totally unfamiliar with the writings of Benedict XV but less so with those of Pius XI, both of whom are arguably two of the most overlooked and underappreciated Popes of the modern era.

Benedict XV

Historians regard Benedict XV as the "Pope of Peace." His pontificate lasted only eight years, ending on January 22, 1922 – and was severely marred by the bloody World War I and its hellish aftermath even as Czarist Russia and the Austro-Hungarian Empire collapsed – the latter with the overthrow of the Hapsburg, Charles I of Austria, who is now a candidate for canonization. We can only imagine how those tumultuous times had an impact on Catholic education. But Benedict was stalwart in this regard. Faced with the Russian Revolution in October of 1917 and the Bolshevik overthrow of Tsar Nicholas II, the last of the Romanov dynasty, Pope Benedict "founded a special college for Russian priests and ordered that missionary training be improved. Moreover, he forbade missionaries to act as agents of their countries of origin in the mission field."[1] That Russian College, known as the *Russicum,* still exists in Rome today and, if you pass by it, you will notice the image of the "Little Flower," Patroness of the Missions.

---

[1] Charles A, Coulombe. *Vicars of Christ: A History of the Popes*, 315.

Addressing the "Order of Pious Schools" founded by Saint Joseph Calasanz, who had been falsely accused of sexual abuse of minors and ostracized by members of his own community, Benedict XV, doing a 180-degree turn, compared "the innocence of his [Calasanz's] ways" to those of Saint Aloysius Gonzaga and commended him for choosing Mary, *Sedes Sapientiae* ("Seat of Wisdom"), as the special patroness of the Order. [see pages 11-12][2]

In a Letter to the "Roman Union of Ursuline Virgins," the first female teaching order not bound by the rules of monastic enclosure, founded by Saint Angela Merici, Benedict exhorts the nuns to "pursue with more tenacious zeal in your task educating the mind and hearts of young girls in such a way that they become mothers worthy of their Christian Faith." [see pages 13-14]

---

[2] The bracketed numbers refer to the pages in the Anthology.

Pius XI

Benedict XV's Successor on the Chair of Peter reigned from February 6, 1922, till February 10, 1939. Achille Ratti took the name Pius in honor of Pius IX during whose reign he was born and of Pius X who had facilitated his getting a post in the Vatican's Secretariat of State.

Born into a middle-class family in 1857, his father was a silk weaver; Ratti was raised near Como in Milan's gorgeously scenic and temperate Lake District. George Weigel describes Achille Ratii as a distinguished academic and accomplished alpinist who used to refer to himself jokingly as "part mountain goat."[1]

Like Benedict XV, Pius XI was a champion of peace in his own right, taking as his papal motto: *Pax Christi in Regno Christi* ("The Peace of Christ in the Kingdom of Christ").

Pius XI had a long history in Catholic education. He obtained three doctorates in philosophy, theology, and canon law from the Pontifical Gregorian University; was a former seminary professor in Padua; served as chief librarian at Milan's venerable

---

[1] *The Irony of Modern Catholic History*, 95.

"Ambrosian Library"; and later served as Prefect of the Vatican Library.

He was indeed very keen on Catholic education and spoke up courageously in favor of the rights of Catholic parents to safeguard the authentic Catholic education of their children against secular incursions, such as were taking place in the virulently anti-Catholic and anti-clerical Mexican *Cristeros* War (1926-1929) and the bloody Spanish Civil War (1936-1939). Both wars produced numerous martyrs including priests, religious and even some young children whose last words were: *Viva Cristo Rey!* ("Long Live Christ the King!"). In this historical context, Pius XI instituted the Feast of Christ the King.

Pius XI's courageous defense of Catholic education is enshrined in his Encyclical *Divini Illius Magistri*, promulgated on December 31, 1929. Quoting Saint Augustine of Hippo's famous line from his *Confessions*: "Thou didst create us, O Lord, for Thyself, and our heart is restless til it rests in Thee," Pius XI then comments that "there can be no ideally perfect education which is not Christian education" [see page 21] and, in turn, cites Saint John Chrysostom who writes, "What greater work is there than training the mind and forming the habits of the young?" [see page 22].

Furthermore, the Pontiff, basing his arguments on Sacred Scripture and the Fathers of the Church, in particular the "Great Commission" of Matthew 28 and Saint Augustine's adage, "He has not God for father who refuses to have the Church as mother," solemnly declares the "supernatural motherhood" of the Church as uniquely expressed in Catholic education. Pius XI states to this effect:

> And first of all education belongs preeminently to the Church [...] Hence, with regard to every other kind of human learning and instruction, which is the common patrimony of individuals and society, the Church has an independent right to make use of it, and above all to decide what may help or harm Christian education. And this must be so, because the Church as a perfect society has an independent right to the means conducive to its end [...] [see pages 22 and 23].

Moreover, Pius XI expresses an encomium of Catholic education when he quotes Saint Gregory of

Nazianzen, a fourth-century Cappadocian Father of the Church, who believed that the Christian education of young people constitutes, "the art of arts and the science of sciences." [see page 40].

Relying on the early Christian writer, Tertullian of Carthage, Pius XI wisely admonishes that the "true nature of Christian education" necessarily means being counter-cultural, that is to say, that Catholic parents and students in every age should endeavor to be like the first Christians who learned to be "sharers in the possessions of the world, not of its error." [see page 41]

Coulombe notes in summary fashion: "[...] in this document [*Divini Illius Magistri*] he [Pius XI] declared – as against the Fascists and the Communists – that parents had the primary role in education, followed by the Church, and only lastly by the State."[2] A year later to the day (December 31, 1930), Pius XI promulgated the Encyclical *Casti Connubii* in which he defended the Church's perennial opposition to artificial contraception, championing a comprehensive Catholic theology of marriage, family, and the sanctity of human life.

---

[2] *The Irony of Modern Catholic History*, 318.

Pius XI was a strong supporter of *Azione Cattolica*, the "Catholic Action" movement, which was comprised mainly of youthful Catholic intellectuals. This movement spread rapidly from Italy to other parts of Europe becoming a formidable force of political influence in defense of Catholic doctrine, morality, and social teaching as enunciated in Leo XIII's Encyclical *Rerum Novarum* and Pius XI's own Encyclical *Quadragesimo Anno,* which commemorated the latter's fortieth anniversary, in which Papa Ratti indicated a "third way" or *via media* between the extremes of Socialism and Capitalism. In effect, "Catholic Action" did a great deal to buoy the Catholic nations of Europe ravaged by World War I.

Permit me to conclude this section on Pius XI by citing his often forgotten Encyclical *Studiorum Ducem*, on "The Law and Method of Following the Doctrine of Saint Thomas Aquinas," promulgated on June 29, 1923. The Pontiff writes several fine lines on Thomism and Thomistic studies, not to mention, "academic freedom":

> We desire very much that those especially who hold the *magisteria* of the highest disciplines in

the schools of the clergy note carefully and observe inviolably all the precepts which both Our predecessors, and first of all Leo XIII and Pius X, have decreed and We ourselves have ordered last year. Moreover, let them be convinced that they will then satisfy the demands of their office and will likewise fulfill Our expectation, if when they begin truly to love the Doctor Aquinas, by a long and intensive study of his works, and by interpreting the Doctor himself, they communicate the warmth of this love to the students under their instruction, and render them capable of exciting a similar zeal in others [...] But let not some exact from others anything more than this which the Church the mistress and mother of all demands of all; for in those matters about which there is wont to be varied opinions among teachers of higher distinction among our Catholic schools no one is to be prevented from following the opinion which seems to him the most probable.[3]

---

[3] As found in Denzinger's *Sources of Catholic Dogma*, 565-66.

Venerable Pius XII

Pius XI was the mentor to the promising Eugenio Pacelli, a regal young priest from a noble Roman family with a long history of service to the Holy See as part of the so-called "Black Nobility." As a matter of fact, as historian Frederick Baumgartner recounts, "A week before Pius died, he said to a secretary that Pacelli 'will make a fine pope.'"[1] and furthermore adds, "Pacelli became Pius XII to honor his predecessor and his commitment to peace."[2]

Pacelli, born in Rome on March 2, 1876, became the first Roman native to be elected Pope since Clement X in 1670. He was ordained priest in 1899. Pacelli was a brilliant student following in the footsteps of his civil lawyer father, Filippo, and graduated from the Pontifical Lateran University with a doctorate in canon law in 1902, after which he began to work in the Vatican's Secretariat of State as an assistant to Cardinal Gaspari. From 1909-1914, Pacelli taught ecclesiastical diplomacy at the prestigious *Accademia* which was founded in

---

[1] "Behind Locked Doors: A History of Papal Elections," 212.

[2] "Behind Locked Doors," 213.

1701 – the same year as Yale University.

Pius XII was elected on his sixty-sixth birthday – March 2, 1939 – and reigned until October 9, 1958. He was the first Secretary of State elected to the papacy since 1667 and chose as his papal motto, *Opus Justitiae Pax* ("Peace is the Work of Justice"). Eamon Duffy remarks about the 259th Successor of Saint Peter: "He [Pius XII] was elected, as everyone knew, to be Pope in a time of total war, a role for which everything about his career – his diplomatic skills, his gift of languages, his sensitivity and intelligence – all equipped him."[3]

Pius XII's discourses on education were thorough and heartfelt. He left no stone unturned, and his grasp of a wide range of topics from the natural sciences to geopolitics is so impressive as to make one perhaps both envious and annoyed at the same time: envious of his sheer wealth of knowledge and annoyed at his overzealous desire to cram into a single discourse as much information as he possibly could on a given topic.

Here is a sampling of Pius XII's philosophy and

---

[3] "Saints and Sinners: A History of the Popes," 345-46.

theology of Catholic education:

(1) In his General Audience on January 31, 1940, Pius XII extols the exemplary life of Saint John Bosco, who was often the object of ridicule and persecution at the hands of his contemporaries, including fellow priests and religious, which is so inexorably linked to the education of young people, especially wayward boys on the mean streets of industrial Turin in the nineteenth century. In so doing, Papa Pacelli acknowledges Don Bosco's fervent love of the Blessed Virgin Mary and the Holy Eucharist ("The Divine Host") as tied to his mysterious dream of "two columns to which the souls of his students were thrown up against like fragile ships in a tempestuous sea of the world where they had strongly to anchor themselves in order to find salvation and peace." [see page 50]

Pope Pius immediately adds the following commentary: "Religion is therefore the first foundation of a good education. But to it Don Bosco wanted to associate reason,

reason enlightened by the Faith [...]." [see page 50]

(2) On May 19, 1946, Pius XII addresses the Religious Women, Alumnae and Teachers of the "Institute of the Assumption," in which he summarizes the significance of the educational apostolate of the Institute as follows: "To take control of the education of young women and to form them for the family, for the people, for the Church as women capable of corresponding, in virtue of their faith, to the demands of their time: this was the ideal to which Maria Eugenia of Jesus looked; this was the work that she accomplished." [see page 61]

(3) Paying homage to the memory of his venerable Predecessor, Leo XII, Pius XII lauds the noble figure of Saint Frances Xavier Cabrini, the first naturalized American citizen to be canonized, in an address on her "Heroic Figure," delivered on July 9, 1946. In that address the Pontiff underscores the meaning of the adage, "Man disposes, God disposes!" or, perhaps more colloquially, "If you want to make God laugh, then tell Him your

plans!" when he notes historically that, "Frances had dreamed about the whole Far East. But God overturned her plans, and the whole West, the Far West above all, from one pole to the other, became the vast continent of her apostolate." [see page 61]

(4) In an "Address to the Participants of the First National Congress of the Italian Association of Catholic Teachers," delivered on September 8, 1946, Pope Pius XII cites the Encyclical *Divini Illius Magistri* of Pius XI in which he reiterates certain fundamental principles of Catholic teaching regarding the rights of parents to educate their children without undue interference of the State. However, from Pope Pius XII's perspective, the family of the Church has a super-eminent, indeed divine, mission to educate children insofar as she is the "supernatural Teacher and Mother of souls, to whom is entrusted the religious care of humanity, and who therefore is also responsible for the spiritual and moral formation of the young person." [see pages 64 and 65]

To this end, Pius XII exhorts the Catholic teachers: "Let the child grow in the pure surrounding of the Christian family, and give the child a school, that, in concert with the paternal home and with the Church, would work for the healthy formation of young people." [see pages 64 and 65]

(5) Pius XII was truly a man rooted in the concrete circumstances of his age, as well as quite prescient with regards to our own. He understood, for example, the benefits and dangers of technology vis-à-vis not only man's educational progress but likewise his rightly ordered use of material goods and pursuit of happiness and existential welfare in the context of a just and equitable society subordinate to God's plan for our eternal salvation.

Thus, in an "Address on the Occasion of the 80th Anniversary of the Youth of Italian Catholic Action," delivered on September 12, 1948, the Pontiff forewarns that the misuse of technology is akin to setting society ablaze with an uncontrollable and destructive fire. In particular, Pius XII cautions that God's gift of technology – if it falls into the hands of violent men and totalitarian states – can end up being "a terrible instrument of injustice, slavery, cruelty, and causes an increase in modern wars even to the point of intolerable sufferings and torments of peoples." Pius XII counterbalances this statement with another just as relevant today as it was then: "When technology, however, is held and directed by a human society that fears God, that fulfills His precepts and esteems spiritual, moral and eternal realities incomparably more than material realities, then this technology can bring about those benefits, to which it is called according to the designs of the Creator." [see pages 72 and 73]

(6) Pius XII took a holistic approach to Catholic education, regarding it as integrated into the fabric of daily life and as a bulwark of the Christian family against materialism, secularism and otherwise self-centered, godless behavior that divorces believers, especially young people, from a firm and reasonable faith and creates angst and even despair – altogether contrary to Christian joy and flourishing according to the Gospel of Jesus

Christ and the teachings of Holy Mother Church.

Consequently, in an "Address to the Women of Catholic Action Gathered in Rome to Celebrate the 40th Anniversary of their Sodality," delivered on July 14, 1949, Papa Pacelli mentions several key aspects of a proper Christian education and upbringing, which is the goal both of teachers and parents. The Pontiff remarks that it is not enough merely to display crucifixes and sacred images in the classroom if the teachers do not likewise catechize the children as to their theological and spiritual meaning or what he terms "their true sense [...] focused on an intense and solid faith, at whose center are found the great religious truths." [see page 78]

Pope Pius XII also especially emphasizes the duty of parents to pray with their children and model for them fidelity to the Third Commandment (Mass Attendance on Sundays and holy days of obligation); set an example of how to avoid disrespectful language when it "deals with religion and the

Church"; and how to create a domestic environment which promotes the virtues of "peacefulness and diligence; honest, loyal, irreproachable conduct of life." [see page 78]

(7) Almost echoing Saint John Henry Newman's motto of *solus cum solo* – whose works Pius XII enjoyed reading and cherished by keeping copies in his private library – and anticipating the language of the Second Vatican Council in documents like *Gaudium et Spes* and *Dignitatis Humanae*, Papa Pacelli in a "Radio Message – on the Occasion of the 'Day of the Family,'" held on March 23, 1952, speaks at great length not only about the conscience as man's "most intimate and secret nucleus," in other words, as God's own "sanctuary" within the human person, but also of the necessity for the formation of a Christian conscience so that man's proper exercise of free will can help conform his particular actions to the will of God and the life of Christ, who is the Way, the Truth and the Life, not just for Christians but all men. [see pages 96 and 97]

Pius XII elucidates further: "Conscience

is therefore, to say it with an image as ancient as it is worthy, a sanctuary, at whose threshold all must stop; also, if one is dealing with a child, the father and the mother. Only the priest enters there as the curator of souls and minister of the Sacrament of Penance nor for this reason does conscience cease to be the jealous sanctuary, concerning which God Himself wants safeguarded the secretness with the seal of the most sacred silence." [see page 96]

(8) On January 12, 1954, speaking in Spanish via Radio Vatican, Pius XII addressed participants in the "Fifth Inter-American Congress of Catholic Education," focused on the nature of Catholic education in the "New World." Once again, the Supreme Pontiff expressly manifests the continuity between his Magisterium and that of his "unforgettable Predecessor," Pius XI, who taught in his Encyclical *Divini Illius Magistri*, n. 88,

> Perfect schools are the result not so much of good methods as of good teachers, teachers who are thoroughly pre-

> pared and well-grounded in the matter they have to teach; who possess the intellectual and moral qualifications required by their important office; who cherish a pure and holy love for the youths confided to them, because they love Jesus Christ and His Church. [see page 131]

Pius XII goes on to praise the educational and evangelizing efforts of numerous Latin American bishops and saints, including the famous catechist, Saint Turibius of Mongrovejo in Perù, and the Jesuit emancipator of slaves, Saint Peter Claver.

Furthermore, Pius XII was a self-taught Renaissance man who pined for knowledge in every field of human endeavor but always with a view to integrating that humanistic or secular knowledge into a cohesive framework of authentic Catholic faith and devotion as the Fathers and Doctors of the Church did so admirably. Pacelli could often be found sitting amidst the Vatican's library stacks taking notes on books he was researching in preparation for a sermon or address.

In his book, *Absolute Power: How the Pope Became the Most Influential Man in the World*, Paul Collins relates on pages 160 and 161, with a bit of an edge:

> For the last decade of his life, the pope seemed besotted with the necessity of pontificating on everything, and he became preoccupied with studying issues in encyclopedias and books about which he had previously known nothing, so that he could speak about them as though he were an expert. It was as though he could not bear to think there was anything upon which he could not pontificate authoritatively. The extraordinary range of topics he covered is recorded in the volumes of the Vatican yearbook, the *Acta Apostolicae Sedis* for 1940 to 1958 on the Holy See website. Examples of the groups he addressed are as diverse as scientists, analgesia specialists, bankers, engineers, architects, the Roman Rota, university professors,

foundry technicians, cardinals, accountants, the Food and Agricultural Organization, Catholic young women (on the need for female modesty), priests, students, academics, Bavarian hoteliers, artists from the Comédie Française, and, perhaps most famous of all, Italian midwives, whom he lectured at length on periodic abstinence [...] Tablet editor Douglas Wooddruf says that he wanted to "address every organized calling before he died, among the last were book stall keepers, bee keepers and plastic surgeons."

It should be noted that Pius XII had ruminated about the possibility of convoking his own Vatican II but was ultimately dissuaded from doing so. We can only imagine how the Church and the Sacred Liturgy would look today had the 21st Ecumenical Council taken place on Papa Pacelli's watch. Charles Coulombe offers this sobering coda on Pius XII's life: "By the end of his Pontificate, Pius apparently despaired of the future of orthodoxy, being quoted in his *Life* magazine obituary as saying that he would be 'the last' Pope to hold the entirety of the Catholic Faith."[4]

---

[4] "Vicars of Christ: A History of the Popes," 323.

Saint John XXIII

Before entering the diplomatic service of the Holy See and being consecrated a bishop on the Feast of Saint Joseph, March 19, 1925, Father (later Monsignor) Roncalli served as a professor of History and Patristics in a diocesan seminary, and during World War I from 1915-1918 as a reserve hospital orderly and army chaplain, whereby he befriended soldiers and even brought many of them back to the Faith. In 1921, Roncalli accepted an assignment from Pope Benedict XV to coordinate the Papal Missionaries in Italy, befriending the Father General of the PIME Fathers to whom he often turned for counsel and advice. Thus, Roncalli developed a life-long love for the Church's foreign missions.

His keen love of history was evident throughout his entire life as he never stopped researching a topic very dear to his head and heart, namely, the life and times of Saint Charles Borromeo, Cardinal-Archbishop of Milan, who was the most outstanding luminary of the Catholic Counter-Reformation and arguably the most noteworthy bishop of his time to have implemented with great zeal the decrees of the Council of Trent.

As a pastor of souls, Father Roncalli followed the "principle of gradualism" in moral theology, taught by the likes of Saint Alphonsus Liguori, which meant that he did not expect penitents to go from vice to virtue overnight. Furthermore, Father Roncalli, the future Patriarch of Venice, believed that it behooved a priest to be "a lion in the pulpit but a lamb in the confessional," following the advice of Saint Augustine of Hippo. He also applied to his pastoral work a principle found in Saint Francis de Sales' classic work, *Introduction to a Devout Life*, namely, that it is easier to attract souls to Christ with honey than vinegar, that is to say, by exhibiting kindness rather than harshness when dealing with sinners.

Starting in 1895, Roncalli began keeping a spiritual diary which he entitled, "Journey of a Soul." Today, this is a classic of Christian spirituality in its own right. In his diary, the Pope admits, "My own temperament inclines me towards compliance and a readiness to appreciate the good side of people and things, rather than to criticize and pronounce harsh judgments."

Good Pope John XXIII's discourses gave me the impression that he enjoyed engaging his audiences in a *cor ad cor loquitur* ("Heart speaks to heart") – Newman's cardinatial motto, first coined by Saint Augustine and later adopted by Saint Francis de Sales. By this, I mean that John XXIII sometimes opted to speak off the cuff, rather than strictly following a prepared text. This spontaneity was evident during his unforgettable *Discorso alla Luna* ("Discourse to the Moon"), in which he tenderly told the parents in Saint Peter's Square that they should go home and give their children a hug and a kiss on his behalf and in the historic back-to-back visits to Rome's children's hospital *Bambino Gesù* and *Regina Caeli* prison, both of which are still extant, on Christmas Day and Saint Stephen's Day, respectively in 1958.

To comprehend John XXIII's pedagogy, one must be aware of his inter-religious and ecumenical sensitivity, which was a fruit of his diplomatic work with Eastern Orthodox Christians and Muslims in Bulgaria, Turkey, and Greece. Furthermore, as James Hitchcock explains, John XXIII believed that the Second Vatican Council would constitute a

"New Pentecost," better equipping the Church in the modern age to evangelize the nations. Hitchcock therein also notes: "He hoped for nothing less than the conversion of the world, something that required Catholics to put aside the defensiveness that had characterized the Church since the Counter-Reformation."[1]

As to the accusation of Liberalism, Hitchcock furthermore notes that in his Apostolic Constitution *Veterum Sapientia* ("The Wisdom of the Ancients"), promulgated on February 22, 1962, Pope John XXIII mandated that all seminary classes be taught in Latin[2] and that the schemata which he had Cardinal Alfredo Ottaviani (Head of the Holy Office of the Inquisition, renamed by Paul VI as the Congregation for the Doctrine of the Faith) prepare for Vatican II were of unquestionable orthodoxy.

Unfortunately, his Latin mandate was dead on arrival, as were likewise many of his conservative

---

[1] "History of the Catholic Church," 475.

[2] John XXIII appreciated Latin as the Church's universal tongue, an expression of its inherent "catholicity." He believed that Latin's precision as a "dead language" to be most suitable for teaching immutable doctrines.

pastoral decrees (e.g., priests had to wear cassocks in public) emanating from the Synod of the Diocese of Rome which he had convoked as a trial balloon for Vatican II, one that burst almost immediately, acting in the minds of many Vatican insiders as an ominous harbinger of things to come.

Given the brevity of John XXIII's reign, there is a paucity of his material on Catholic education in our anthology. Of the texts provided, the one that I felt had the greatest import was the homily he preached on March 17, 1963, for the beatification of Elizabeth Ann Bayley Seton, whom the Pontiff identifies as "justly considered one of the founders of the parochial school system, that has produced much fruit and continues to do so in the United States, offering to the Church and to the nations ranks of fervent Catholics and exemplary citizens." [see pages 146 and 147]

Pope John XXIII concludes his homily with a beautiful prayer directly invoking the new blessed:

> O Blessed Elizabeth Seton, who stands out today in the sight of the nations for your fidelity to your baptismal promises, look with an eye of

love at your people, who glory in you as the first fruit of sanctity. Obtain from God the grace to safeguard the sacred patrimony of the Gospel call, firmness of faith, ardor in charity, so that your people may joyfully correspond to their particular vocation. And over the entire Church extend your protection, offering to her an example of the fire of generosity and love, that compelled you to move from glory to glory (2 Corinthians 3:18) until your glorification today! [see page 147]

Saint Paul VI

Giovanni Battista Montini was the son of very intelligent and proactive Catholic parents. Montini's mother was a schoolteacher of minor nobility; his father was a wealthy landowner, well-respected lawyer, editor of a Catholic newspaper, and a leader in *Azione Cattolica*.

As a young priest, Father Montini, due to chronic health problems, received a rare dispensation to obtain a doctorate from the Pontifical Gregorian University without having to live in Rome. He was actively involved in the *Federation of Italian Catholic Universities* (F.U.C.I).

The fact that during the Jubilee Year of the Redemption in 1975 Paul VI canonized Saint Elizabeth Ann Seton, the foundress of the parochial school system in the United States and America's first native-born Saint, should strike us not as coincidental but rather as deliberately emblematic of the Pontiff's tireless commitment to Catholic education.

Our anthology [see pages 148-215] provides numerous texts exemplary of Pope Paul VI's deep appreciation of Catholic education, not only as a special vehicle for the transmission of knowledge but as a powerful catalyst for cultivating the highest forms of human culture and the most profound formation of the human person within the context of a civilization of truth and love and the superabundant life of the Holy Mother Church ever focused on man's sanctification and eternal salvation. Permit me to highlight six of my favorite texts.

(1) In his "Address to the Italian Catholic University Federation," on September 2, 1973, he exhorts:

> [...] We would like moreover to recommend that you take to heart the Catholic culture. You can, first and foremost, explore its treasures: one of the deplorable lacunae of contemporary culture is the ignorance of religious truths, especially in their authentic formulation, their sources, the traditional patrimony of Catholic thought, and the expressions of the Ecclesiastical Magisterium. This la-

cuna can be filled by the study of religion, made a precious and integral element of university study. [see page 149]

(2) On September 26, 1963, Pope Paul VI sent a Message to Georgetown University on the occasion of its 175th Anniversary. The Pontiff reflects on the example of the Jesuit priests and Brothers, collectively known as the North American Martyrs, whose sacrifice helped plant the seed of the Gospel in the "infant Church," of the North American Continent. Paul VI points out that 1789 was the year in which the United States adopted its Constitution and Georgetown University was founded by Jesuit Father John Carroll, thus making Georgetown – in the words of Papa Montini – "the Alma Mater of Catholic Colleges in the United States of America." [see pages 150 and 151]

(3) Paul VI's Radio Message "to the Catholic school children of the United States of America" on February 12, 1964, occurred on Ash Wednesday and so afforded him an opportunity to link Catholic education to the

sacred disciplines of Lent: prayer, fasting and almsgiving. While acknowledging the material advances of children in the prosperous United States, the Pontiff brings the children's attention to less fortunate children around the world, "who are undergoing many sufferings" like poverty, hunger, disease, and the disastrous effects of war, which leave too many of them homeless and even orphaned. In this context, Paul VI praises the work of "Catholic Relief Services," "through which they give assistance to these needy children," setting an example for all "generous Catholic people in order to continue this noble work." The Pope then exhorts the Catholic school children "to make in the spirit of Lent, your little sacrifices to bring aid and comfort to those in distress [...] to help your bishops to aid these poor children of the world." [see pages 153 and 154]

(4) In an "Address to the International Federation of 'Pueri Cantores'" on April 9, 1964, Paul VI offers these words of sincere en-

couragement:

> [...] May they know that their activity, meant to join the voices of children to the celebration of liturgical rites and to the execution of sacred song, is very much appreciated by Us, not only for its characteristic innocence, freshness and beauty that the participation of the "Pueri Cantores," introduces into the sacred ceremonies and offers to the Christian people, but likewise on account of the exquisite homage that is thus lifted up to the Lord, by the vital and gentle piety which it introduces into public worship, and through the best observance of the criteria and norms emanating from the Constitution on the Sacred Liturgy of the Second Ecumenical Vatican Council. [see pages 161 and 162]

(5) In his November 12, 1964, address on the "Fourth Centenary of the Birth of William Shakespeare," Pope Paul VI underscores

how the writings of the great English bard are of significance to the Roman people, as well as through their artistic collaborations with various elements of the "British Catholic Communities" in the Eternal City. Paul VI mentions how, in 1934, he made a trip "as an enquiring and hasty tourist" to Shakespeare's hometown of Stratford-on-Avon where he experienced firsthand "the work of the great poet," which Romans and all peoples should honor and esteem as "the high achievement of the human spirit," of the "supreme writer" whose plays and sonnets constitute "the magnificent cultural tradition and artistic genius of the English people." The Pontiff waxes eloquently and continues thus:

> We take especial pleasure in noting how the profound humanity of Shakespeare, ever open to adventurous and poetic exploration, leads us to the discovery of moral laws which make life great and sacred, and leads us back to a religious un-

derstanding of the world. His lofty genius and powerful language induces men to listen with reverence to the great verities he expounds, of death and judgment, of hell and heaven. The plots of his plays are a salutary reminder to modern man that God exists, that there is a life after this life, that evildoing is punished and good rewarded. Our enjoyment of the poet's vision of humanity should not make us overlook the high moral lessons and admonitions contained in his works." [see page 166][1]

(6) Expounding on the evangelical message of "The Golden Rule," as set forth in Matthew 25:40, on March 21, 1964, Paul VI encouraged "The Italian Association of Catholic Teachers" not merely "to serve the needs of others" but to love their neighbor by recognizing Jesus "mysteriously" present in them.

---

[1] It would undoubtedly gladden the heart of Paul VI to learn of a literary consensus today which holds that Shakespeare was a Catholic!

The Pontiff then rhapsodizes:

> Oh, how the Catholic teacher knows and experiences these canons of charity! And We can moreover say to you, Catholic Teachers, that the Church also needs you; also the Church calls you to the grand and the austere, and often neglected, academic duty; wherever exercised, it is sublime; also the Church corroborates in you the certitude of having chosen an optimal road, life has reached you in its most generous and most sacred expressions; also the Church consoles your dedication with the promise of recompense, which goes beyond the economic remuneration and the temporal advantages of an honored profession; recall: "You have done it unto me," the Lord will say on the Last Day for every humble concern addressed to "my little ones." [see page 157]

Blessed John Paul I

Papa Luciani, like Papa Montini, was extremely well-educated and was an effective catechist and educator in his own right. After finishing his doctorate in sacred theology at the Pontifical Gregorian University in 1947, the last Pope to graduate from "The Greg," Luciani not only participated in all four sessions of Vatican II as the Bishop of Vittorio Veneto, whence he condemned the Communist-tinged "Worker-Priest Movement," so popular in France and parts of Northern Italy, but also wrote a work entitled *Catechetica in briciole* ("Catechesis in Crumbs"), published in 1949. This book was inspired by his participation in the 1949 Eucharistic Congress held in the Diocese of Belluno and was aimed at simplifying catechetical lessons for less educated Catholics.

In 1971, Luciani was personally invited by Paul VI to attend the worldwide Synod of Bishops, during which he gave an address in which he said that the wealthy nations of the world should give one percent of their Gross Domestic Product (GDP) to the poorer nations. Two years later (1973), Paul VI created Luciani a cardinal. In the interim,

Luciani served on the doctrinal committee of the Italian Episcopal Conference (CEI) and from 1972 to 1975 as its Vice President.

In 1978, shortly before his papal election, Cardinal Luciani wrote a series called *Illustrissimi* ("The Illustrious Ones"), a compilation of essays in the form of letters, in which Luciani addressed historical figures like King David, Jesus, Saint Teresa of Avila, Goethe, Charles Dickens and Mark Twain, as well as fictional characters like Pinocchio and those featured in Dickens' *The Pickwick Papers*. He wrote these letters not primarily to express his literary erudition and creativity but pedagogically to introduce young people to the lives of famous people who had left indelible marks on Western culture and civilization.

As Pope, whose reign lasted a mere thirty-three days, he managed to preside at three Wednesday audiences, whose themes were the theological virtues of faith, hope and charity. During those audiences, John Paul I was self-deprecating, stating that he possessed neither the expansive humanity of John XXIII nor the theological preparedness of Paul VI. And yet, week after week in September of 1978, this shy and retiring man entered into the packed *Aula Nervi* (Paul VI Auditorium), carried on the *sedia gestatoria* – the last Pope to use it – so that he could be seen by the large crowds and lay bare his pastoral heart, revealing his own humble *humanitas*.

At those few audiences, Luciani quoted verbatim from memory the Roman poet Trilussa, who wrote in Roman dialect not standard Italian, and to interact in such a gentle and tender fashion with the little children in the audience, including a choir boy from Malta named James, whom he spontaneously called up to the papal platform to participate in a question-and-answer dialogue about the virtues.

In his General Audience of September 6, 1978, John Paul I cites Bishop Bossuet: "Where no one commands, everyone commands. Where everyone commands, no one commands any longer, but chaos." The purpose of this quote was to underscore the importance of children obeying their parents as a virtuous exercise of both justice and charity. Herein the Pontiff defines charity as the "soul of justice."

In his second General Audience on September 13, 1978, Papa Luciani reflected on the gift of faith as one of "The Seven Lamps of Sanctification," the title of a retreat which he once preached and whose publication was acknowledged by Pope John XXIII. For Pope John Paul I, the "Seven Lamps of Sanctification" include the three theological virtues of faith, hope, and charity and the four cardinal virtues of prudence, justice, fortitude, and temperance. The Pontiff instructs us that some truths of the Faith are "pleasant," while others are "unpalatable to our spirit." And yet, because God can neither deceive nor be deceived, we have reason enough to trust His word and to put our personal faith in Him as we would in our own good parents.

Since Saint Paul clearly taught that the Church is the Mystical Body of Christ, it is a lame and futile excuse to cling to what we would term the distinction between being "spiritual but not religious," which many an agnostic, evangelical-fundamentalist or fallen-away Catholic faint-heartedly espouses today as a defensive mantra. Papa Luciani firmly declares to the contrary: "It is not possible to have faith and to say, 'I believe in Jesus. I accept Jesus but I do not accept the Church.' We must accept the Church, as she is. And what is the Church like? Pope John Paul I called her, *'Mater et Magistra.'*

Teacher also. St. Paul said, 'Let everyone accept us as Christ's aides and stewards and dispensers of His mysteries.' When the poor Pope, when the bishops, the priests, propose the doctrine, they are merely helping Christ. It is not our doctrine, it is Christ's; we must just guard it and present it." [see page 220]

His third General Audience, held on September 20, 1978, was focused on the theological virtue of hope, "the second of the seven 'Lamps of Sanctification.'" In his talk, John Paul I refers to the great Italian poet Dante and the Angelic Doctor, Saint Thomas Aquinas, not to mention Saint Augustine, Saint Francis de Sales, and even the millionaire tycoon, Andrew Carnegie of Pittsburgh.

Citing Dante's *Divine Comedy*, *il Paradiso* (Cantos 24, 25 and 26), the Pontiff recalls how "Dante imagined himself taking an examination in Christianity. A magnificent commission was operating. 'Do you have faith?' St. Peter asks him first. 'Do you have hope?' St. James continues, 'Do you have charity?' St. John ends. 'Yes,' Dante answers, 'I have faith, I have hope, I have charity.' He proves it and passes with full marks."

Regarding Saint Thomas, Pope John Paul I notes

how the Dominican saint in his *Summa Theologica* included "cheerfulness" (in Latin, *iucunditas*) as a virtue since it signifies "the capacity of changing things heard and seen into a cheerful smile – to the extent and in the way appropriate." John Paul I adds this personal and jocular note: "This kind of cheerfulness, I explained to my pupils, was shown by that Irish mason who fell from the scaffolding and broke his legs. He was taken to the hospital and the doctor and the Sister-nurse rushed to him. 'Poor thing,' the latter said, 'you hurt yourself falling.' But the patient said: 'Mother, not exactly falling, but reaching the ground I hurt myself.'" [see pages 221-223]

In his final General Audience, held on September 27, 1978, Pope John Paul I reflects on the theological virtue of charity, love of God and neighbor. He cites Thomas à Kempis' classic work *Imitation of Christ*, in which he says, "He who loves *"currit, volat, laetatur"* ("runs, flies and rejoices)." Furthermore, the Pontiff teaches: "To love God is therefore a journeying with one's heart to God," adding his signature touch of personal warmth, culture and humanity when he relates,

"When I was a boy, I was thrilled by the journeys described by Jules Verne (*"Twenty Thousand Leagues Under the Sea,"* *"From the Earth to the Moon,"* *"Round The World in Eighty Days,"* etc). But the journeys of love for God are far more interesting. You read them in the lives of the saints. Saint Vincent de Paul, whose feast we celebrate today, for example, is a giant of charity; he loved God more than a father and a mother, and he himself was a father for prisoners, sick people, orphans and the poor. Saint Peter Claver, dedicating himself entirely to God, used to sign: Peter, the slave of the Negroes forever."

John Paul's teaching methods did not sit well with refined *Curialisti* and *Vaticanisti*, who openly criticized the Pontiff, verbally and in writing, for being too informal and superficial in his Magisterium. Still others in the Catholic world questioned the Pope's orthodoxy when he publicly congratulated the mother of the first test-tube baby, Louise Brown, and also spoke of God as our Mother. These criticisms weighed heavily on John Paul I, but he would not live long enough to address them. His untimely death is still shrouded in mystery and is a frequent topic of discussion on Italian television.

Saint John Paul II

John Paul II, the first non-Italian Pope since the Dutchman Adrian VI (1522-1523), was elected to replace Papa Luciani on October 16, 1978. John Paul II was steeped in Catholic education and proudly Polish. His godly parents, who died prematurely, were his primary educators in the Faith. Born on May 18, 1920, in Wadowice, Poland, young Karol Wojtyła would often find his beloved father kneeling in prayer at his bedside. Together they shared a deep Catholic culture and religious piety, especially Eucharistic and Marian, which were put to the test by the evils of Nazism and Communism, so much so that the highly intellectual Karol was forced to work in a quarry and had to flee underground to practice his beloved poetry and acting as well as to be ordained. In 1946, Wojtyła was priested in the secret seminary belonging to the Archdiocese of Cracow, led by Adam Cardinal Sapieha, his dear professor and mentor.

As a priest, Father Karol likewise flourished as a teacher and mentor to young people. He loved to spend time with them both inside and outside the classroom. He never missed an opportunity to teach them about the truths of the Faith, even if just by his "ministry of presence."

Young people greatly appreciated his genuine manliness, sincerity, and charisma. The ladies took a shine to his charm, good looks, and winsome smile. He was arguably the best-looking pontiff since the ruddy Pius X. All were enamored of his formidable language ability, keen wit, sense of humor, and natural way of relating to them based on his own powerful experiences.

They identified with the suffering he endured after the early loss of his beloved parents and elder brother, Edmund, who was a physician; his sacrificing to aid and befriend persecuted Polish Jews; studying philosophy at the prestigious Jagiellonian University and theology at the Pontifical University of Saint Thomas in the City of Rome, more commonly known as the *Angelicum* in honor of Saint Thomas Aquinas, the Dominican "Angelic Doctor"; his brilliant lectures in philosophy as Professor at the Catholic University of Lublin; his philosophical masterpiece, *The Acting Person*, published in 1969; his predilection for reciting poetry and acting; his talent as a playwright (See, "The Jeweler's Shop");

his natural athleticism in swimming, playing soccer, skiing, hiking and kayaking, the last, sometimes with Breviary or shaver in hand as charming old photos reveal.

Above all else, they admired his abiding love of Christ, the Church and the Priesthood which was always evident in his robust preaching and reverent *ars celebrandi* ("art of celebrating") the Sacred Liturgy.

In the early 1980s, John Paul II, ever the "Phenomenological Realist" who, unlike Paul VI, preferred *Realpolitik* to *Ostpolitik*, negotiated new treaties between the Holy See and the Italian government, according to which the salaries of the clergy would no longer be paid by the secular state as long as priests were allowed to continue weekly catechetical instruction in Italy's public schools – an arrangement that persists to this day.

Saint John Paul II's pontificate of nearly 27 years was the third longest in history, after those of Saint Peter and Leo XIII. Its impact was so awesome as to recall the pontificates of Leo the Great (5th c.) and Gregory the Great (6th c.). John Paul II who, at age 58 was the youngest pope elected since Pope Saint

Pius X (1903-1914), demonstrated time and again that Catholic education was a *sine qua non* of the Church's mission and identity. Indeed, as John Paul II was wont to point out, especially during "World Youth Day," an event he initiated in 1985 at the Palm Sunday Mass in Rome, that young people are the future of the Church.

> (1) In his address "To the Bishops of New Zealand" for their November 13, 1978 *Ad Limina* visit, he exhorted the bishops from the "Land Down Under" with these encouraging words:
>
>> In particular I am one with you in your mission of defending human life in all its stages. In all your catechetical endeavors, in all your works for Catholic education, you can count on the solidarity of the universal Church. What an important work it is to provide children with Catholic schools, in which they can 'grow up in every way into him who is the head, into Christ'! What a great challenge it is

for a bishop to guard the deposit of Christian doctrine, so that each new generation can receive the fullness of the apostolic faith! [See page 232]

(2) On the occasion of the 150th anniversary of the birth of the Founder of the Congregation of Saint Joseph, Saint Leonard Murialdo, whom John Paul called a "great educator like Don Bosco," he turns his final thoughts to the Blessed Virgin Mary and young people:

> We cannot conclude without addressing the Blessed Virgin, so loved and venerated by Murialdo, who had recourse to her as the Universal Mediatrix of all grace. The thought of Mary returned continually in his letters. In them he inculcated the recitation of the Rosary, entrusted his Sons with spreading devotion to the Holy Virgin, and stated: 'If one wishes to do a little good among the young, one must instill love for Mary in them.' The beneficial work carried out by your

Founder, is the best confirmation of this. So follow his example in this matter too. [See page 240]

(3) On April 16, 1979, Pope John Paul II addressed the National Catholic Educational Association of the United States, in which he ratified and reaffirmed the words of Pope Paul VI to the American bishops on Catholic education, adding:

> Yes, the Catholic school must remain a privileged means of Catholic education in America. As an instrument of the apostolate it is worthy of the greatest sacrifices. But no Catholic school can be effective without dedicated Catholic teachers, convinced of the great ideal of Catholic education [...] In order that the Catholic school and the Catholic teachers may truly make their irreplaceable contribution to the Church and to the world, the goal of Catholic education itself must be crystal clear. Beloved sons

and daughters of the Catholic Church, brothers and sisters in the faith: Catholic education is above all a question of communicating Christ, of helping to form Christ in the lives of others [...] The cause of Catholic education is the cause of Jesus Christ and of his Gospel at the service of man." [See pages 256 and 257]

(4) Addressing high school students in the Archdiocese of New York on October 3, 1979, Pope John Paul II, during his first of many apostolic journeys to the United States of America, spoke these stirring words:

Be always grateful to God for this gift of knowing Christ. Be grateful also to your parents and to the community of the Church for making possible through many sacrifices, your Catholic education. People have placed a lot of hope in you, and they now look forward to your collaboration in giving witness to Christ, and in transmitting the Gospel to others. The world needs you, because it needs Christ, and you belong to Christ. And so I ask you to accept your responsibility in the Church, the responsibility of your Catholic education: to help – by your words, and, above all, by the example of your lives – to spread the Gospel. You do this by praying, and by being just and truthful and pure.

Dear young people: by a real Christian life, by the practice of your religion you are called to give witness to your faith. And because actions speak louder than words, you are called to proclaim, by the conduct of your daily lives that you really do believe that Jesus Christ is Lord! [See pages 266 and 267]

(5) Addressing the Brothers of the Christian Schools, more commonly known as the Christian Brothers, founded by Saint John Baptiste de la Salle and who taught me in high school, Pope John Paul II proffers an extensive quote from the Second Vatican Council's document on Catholic education entitled, *Gravissimum Educationis* n. 8, couched by the following exhorta-

tion: "Be faithful to the charism of your Institute, be faithful to your original vocation as 'apostles of the school.' A vocation that is truly arduous, which requires renunciation and sacrifice, total dedication to the mission of education, inexhaustible trust in young people and a great love for the Lord, nourished in assiduous prayer, because 'it is God who grants the increase' (cf. 1 Corinthians 3:7)." [See page 273].

(6) On the feast of the Holy Innocents, December 28, 1981, Pope John Paul II gave a talk to the 35th Assembly of the Foundation of the Institutes of Educational Activities, in which he links Catholic education, "its educational ideal and strength of action," to the mystery of the Nativity teaching:

> It must place Jesus Christ and his message of salvation at the foundation of its vision of life. In this way, the Catholic school, without denying its own proper nature as a school destined for the instruction of all that is knowable, would pursue its end in the Christian vision of reality, by means of

which culture achieves its privileged place in the integral vocation of man. May the school know how to mature the aptitudes innate in each young person in the light of various familial, moral and social situations; may it know how to direct the young person to make good choices. A school that would offer, purely and without superficiality, the values that refer to the Gospel and to the perennial teachings of the Church [...] [See page 280].

The Holy Father concludes his talk with laudatory and sagacious words of paternal encouragement and magisterial advice, relevant to all teachers in every time and place:

> Dear brothers and sisters, continue with courage to be engaged in the teaching of the Church. Do not be discouraged before the inevitable difficulties of various types, nor the last of which is that of a lack of specialized personnel. Be always more aware that among the professions that are worthy of

engaging human existence, your profession has a place of the first order, precisely on account of the relationship that comes to be established with young people who model themselves on your professional richness and most especially on your moral and spiritual behavior. The teacher, in fact, if faithful to his mission, is an authentic benefactor of humanity, as he is likewise a father. This is true above all for one who makes the school into a Christian training ground: for the teacher, among the numerous purposes, education and pedagogical, knows how to value that religious purpose and to thus make his own the words of Saint Paul: 'For I became your father in Christ Jesus through the gospel.' (1 Corinthians 4:13)." [See page 281]

(7) Addressing a group of American bishops during their *Ad Limina* visit on October 28, 1983, Pope John Paul II highlights the impact Catholic education has had on the life of the Church in the United States. He notes how "Catholic education has been a very ef-

fective dimension of evangelization, bringing the Gospel to bear on all facets of life"; that "Catholic education in America can, under God's grace, be credited to a high degree with forming the splendid Catholic laity of America"; and that "Catholic education in your land has also fostered numerous vocations over the years." The Pope concludes, "The achievements of Catholic education in America merit our great respect and admiration." [See page 292].

(8) In a discourse to Representatives of the Italian Catholic Schools given on the feast of Saint Thomas Aquinas, January 28, 1984, John Paul wholeheartedly recommends the example of Saint Thomas as a most excellent "patron of the Catholic school," and therefore an exemplary model of both the Catholic school student and teacher. The saintly Pontiff teaches:

> This great doctor, whose teaching has been so many times praised and recom-

mended by my Predecessors, still today intercedes and is an example for all the members of the Catholic school. In the life and doctrine of Thomas, you will find many inspirational points for realizing the dual dimensions of which I have spoken: service of man and society, and likewise the promotion of faith and the Kingdom of God. You will find the model of the disciple as a Catholic teacher: a Christian who makes conscientious fulfillment of the duties of his proper state of life a "pathway" of the Church, that is to say, a way of divine mercy toward the world. Thomas knew how to make the school the means of an encounter of Christ with man in search of the truth and salvation. Saint Thomas, together with Saint Augustine, maintained that the greatest work of mercy was that of leading the brother from the darkness of ignorance into the light of truth, in which consists the foundation of the dignity and liberty of man. But where did Saint Thomas find the fount of this synthesis between faith and culture, between ecclesial commitment and the service of society? He found it in the profound unity that he knew to create, in his spirit, between the activity of study and search for holiness. [See pages 296 and 297]

(9) In an address to "Parents, Teachers and Students of the Catholic Schools of Lazio" on March 9, 1985, Pope John Paul II reiterates certain basic principles which govern the Church's philosophy of Catholic education: "The parents are the principal educators of their progeny, the first catechists in the service of the transmission of the faith, so that the life of their children would be penetrated from the very beginning by the spirit of Christ." The Polish Pontiff adds: "The family is the privileged place of birth and human and religious growth, the natural school where one has the first experience of community, learning the social virtues, the

sense of God, and love for neighbor." Almost echoing the African proverb about the education of children, namely, "It takes a village!," the Holy Father elucidates further in defense of parental school choice, "But when children are advanced in their development, parents, in order the more adequately to carry out their task, need the help of the entire society; and, in the first place, they must enjoy a real possibility of choice in the field of the school, without further economic burdens." John Paul II concludes this section of his talk by addressing teachers who function *"in loco parentis"* when he states:

> Catholic educators are those who have a more lively awareness of exercising a function of substitute teaching and subsidiarity, entrusted to them by the parents, and, in the fulfillment of a mission that is freely chosen, they feel themselves to be collaborators of the family and the Church. [see page 315]

(10) Almost a year later to the day, on March 9, 1986, Pope John Paul once again addressed the "Students of the Catholic Schools of the Diocese of Rome and of the Region of Lazio" and, in so doing, praised their study of the documents of the Second Vatican Council and the Council's document on Catholic education, *Gravissimum Educationis*. The Holy Father proceeds to cite a key portion of that text which, he asserts, "delineates the profile of the student and at the same time the tasks of the Catholic school."

What is the Pope's ultimate goal in quoting at length from *Gravissimum Educationis* 8? At last, he himself explains: "These are programmatic words, to be kept in mind, so that the Catholic school might be truly a forge of strong, lively, and true personalities, who would know how to radiate without embarrassment the authentic human and Christian values."

Given the import of *Gravissimum Educationis* 8, in and of itself as well as in the magisterium of John Paul, I would like to conclude this section citing those aforementioned "programmatic words" which are in effect paradigmatic for our entire anthology. The 264th Successor of Saint Peter prefaces the quote by saying: "In *Gravissimum Educationis*, one reads, among other things, that upon the school is incumbent the obligation. . . :

> to help young people grow according to the new creatures they were made through baptism as they develop their own personalities, and finally to order the whole of human culture to the news of salvation so that the knowledge the students gradually acquire of the world, life, and man is illumined by faith. So indeed the Catholic school, while it is open, as it must be, to the situation of the contemporary world, leads its students to promote efficaciously the good of the earthly city and also prepares them for service in the spread of the Kingdom of God, so that by leading an

exemplary apostolic life they become, as it were, a saving leaven in the human community. [see page 327]

In fine, it was reported that on his death bed, John Paul II said about the young people gathered in Saint Peter's Square that as he had come in search of them, now they had come in search of him. What more touching words could ever be said to link the papacy and the Catholic education of our youth!

Benedict XVI

John Paul II's right-hand man and trusted Successor on the Chair of Peter, Joseph Cardinal Ratzinger, was for decades affectionately called "The German Shepherd" by Conservatives and nastily dubbed "God's Rottweiler" and "Der Panzer Cardinal" by Liberals.

It is not surprising that this quintessential German (or rather Bavarian!) scholar and professor of theology, whose university lecture halls had been packed to the gills in the 60s and 70s, focused significant portions of his magisterium – profoundly rooted in his Augustinian *Weltanschauung* and the logic of his episcopal motto *"Cooperatores in Veritate"* (Cooperators in the Truth) – on Catholic education.

Moreover, author Joseph Pearce[1] notes that it was a series of Lenten sermons which Cardinal Ratzinger had preached that convinced Pope John Paul II that he was the right man to be the head of the Congregation for the Doctrine of the Faith, beginning in 1981, a post which Ratzinger held until

---

[1] See pages 31, 51-52 of his book *Benedict XVI: Defender of the Faith.*

John Paul II's death in 2005.

Apart from Benedict XVI's lengthy and erudite encyclicals (*Deus Caritas Est*; *Caritas in Veritate* and *Spe Salvi*) and Post-Synodal Apostolic Exhortations (*Verbum Domini*; *Sacramentum Caritatis*) what I found most compelling about Benedict the Educator and Teacher were his recondite homilies.

Several stand out in my mind because I was blessed to hear them in person: his inaugural homily preached in Saint Peter's Square in April of 2005 and the one he preached at Saint Patrick's Cathedral in April of 2008; his homily for Newman's beatification, which Father Stravinskas and I were both fortunate to concelebrate, albeit while sporting plastic ponchos in the pouring rain that drenched Crofton Park.

All of Benedict XVI's homilies were carefully crafted. It is said that the meticulous Benedict XVI would make corrections to his homilies even as he was vested and waiting for the Entrance Procession to begin. This was the professor in him! Benedict XVI was acutely aware of the power of the written and spoken word, especially in his role as Supreme Pontiff. It is no wonder, then, that he dedicated each

Thursday, his "day off," to researching and writing his trilogy, *Jesus of Nazareth*.

As Dean of the College of Cardinals, Ratzinger was tasked with being the main celebrant and homilist of "The Mass for Electing the Roman Pontiff," held on April 18, 2005, prior to the Conclave. In his homily, Ratzinger coined the famous phrase, "The Dictatorship of Relativism," much as John Paul II had coined terms like "The New Evangelization," "The Culture of Death," and "The Culture of Life." Apparently, Ratzinger's homily was so powerful that it moved many of his brother Cardinals to vote for him.

Furthermore, taking my inspiration from George Weigel's excellent book, *The Irony of Modern Catholic History*, I would highlight what Weigel terms Benedict's "September Lectures" as illustrative of the German Pontiff's *Weltanschauung* ("world view") and magisterial aplomb.

The first talk was his controversial "Regensburg Address" on September 12, 2006, which taken out of its scholarly context in the light of September 11, 2001, infuriated Muslims and irked the liberal secular media around the world because he cited a

Byzantine Emperor who, in dialogue with a Persian scholar, questioned the rational nature of Islam as compared to the Christian kerygma.

The second talk was Benedict XVI's September 12, 2008, speech at Paris' *Collège des Bernardins* (a former Benedictine monastery), in which he encouraged the revival of the monastic quest to *quærere Deum* ("to seek God") by returning to the sources of Divine Revelation, especially through the prayerful contemplation of Sacred Scripture, using the method of *Lectio Divina* perfected by the medieval monks. It is not surprising, therefore, that when the naturally shy and recollect Ratzinger was elected pope, he chose to be called Benedict.

His third talk was a stirring speech at London's Westminster Hall on September 17, 2010, as the Pope stood where, centuries earlier, Sir Thomas More had been tried and sentenced to death by King Henry VIII for refusing to rubber-stamp the Tudor King's demands for a papal annulment of his marriage to Catherine of Aragon, so that he could marry his lover, Anne Boleyn, whom he later had executed, as he did another of his six wives; and for refusing to back Henry's "Oath of Supremacy" in defiance of papal authority which, in effect, declared that King Henry VIII was now head of his own church.

Benedict XVI's fourth and final September Lecture was delivered on September 22, 2011, at the German *Bundestag* in Berlin during which he challenged his countrymen with a question taken from Saint Augustine's "City of God": "Without justice – what else is the State but a great band of robbers?"

Lastly, forever etched in my mind is that extraordinary encounter Pope Benedict XVI had with the priests and seminarians of the Diocese of Rome shortly before he resigned and took that sad helicopter ride to bid farewell to the Eternal City even as tearful seminarians stood on the rooftop of the North American College to wave goodbye. Speaking in fluent Italian and without a prepared text, the Holy Father explained the history of the real Vatican II as opposed to "the Council of the Media" and "the Spirit of Vatican II." The Pontiff furthermore explicated the critical importance of affirming "a hermeneutic of continuity," rather than "a hermeneutic of discontinuity/rupture," between the Church of the Second Vatican Council and the Church of the Pre-Vatican II era.

Our anthology can be relied on to underscore Benedict XVI's tremendous appreciation for Catholic education.

In his homily for the Fifth World Meeting of Families, held on July 6, 2006, the Holy Father, referring to the biblical figures of Esther and Saint Paul, exhorts parents to exercise their prophetic role in the family as those principally charged with "the handing on of the faith." Citing *Familiaris Consortio* n. 60 of John Paul II, the German Pontiff teaches:

> The Christian family passes on the faith when parents teach their children to pray and when they pray with them; when they lead them to the sacraments and gradually introduce them to the life of the Church; when all join in reading the Bible, letting the light of faith shine on their family life and praising God as our Father. [498]

Pope Benedict goes on to cite his own homily for the Vigil of Pentecost (June 9, 2006): "The Church does not cease to remind us that true human freedom derives from our having been created in God's image and likeness. Christian education is consequently an education in freedom and for freedom." [498]

During the *Ad Limina* visit of the German bishops on November 10, 2006, Benedict XVI reminded them:

> At Catholic schools, moreover, it is important that the introduction to the Catholic vision of the world and the practice of faith, as well as the integral Catholic formation of the personality be transmitted convincingly, not only during religion classes but indeed, throughout the school day – and not the least through the teacher's personal witness. [501]

On April 17, 2008, Benedict XVI delivered a lengthy address to Catholic educators in our nation's Capital in which he praised the educational vision and apostolic activity of Saints Elizabeth Ann Seton and Katharine Drexel and proceeded to cite Sacred Scripture, Vatican II (e.g., *Gaudium et Spes*, 22), and the writings of John Paul II (e.g., the

Encyclical *Fides et Ratio*) – not to mention the Encyclical *Dei Filius* of Vatican I and his own Encyclical *Spe Salvi* to make several key points. For example, the Holy Father, almost as though he were leading an Examination of Conscience, asks the following questions which he prefaces thus:

> A university or school's Catholic identity is not simply a question of the number of Catholic students. It is a question of conviction – do we really believe that only in the mystery of the Word made flesh does the mystery of man truly become clear (cf. *Gaudium et Spes*, 22)? Are we ready to commit our entire self – intellect and will, mind and heart – to God? Do we accept the truth Christ reveals? Is the faith tangible in our universities and schools? Is it given fervent expression liturgically, sacramentally, through prayer, acts of charity, a concern for justice, and respect for God's creation? Only in this way do we really bear witness to the meaning of who we are and what we uphold. [pg. 507].

Further on, he instructs the Catholic teachers:

Teachers and administrators, whether in universities or schools, have the duty and privilege to ensure that students receive instructions in Catholic doctrine and practice. This requires that public witness to the way of Christ, as found in the Gospel and upheld by the Church's Magisterium, shapes all aspects of an institution's life, both inside and outside the classroom. Divergence from this vision weakens Catholic identity and, far from advancing freedom, inevitably leads to confusion, whether moral, intellectual or spiritual. [510].

On April 19, 2008, I was privileged to attend Pope Benedict XVI's meeting with Young People and Seminarians in the Archdiocese of New York. His words truly resonated with me as a native New Yorker who attended several of the Archdiocese's schools. On that occasion, Benedict XVI lauded the extraordinary holiness of six saintly men and women who "each responded to the Lord's call to a life of charity and each [and] served here, in the alleys, streets and suburbs of New York," alluding to Saint Elizabeth Ann Seton, Saint Frances Xavier

Cabrini, Saint John Neumann, Blessed (now-Saint) Kateri Tekawitha, Venerable Pierre Toussaint and Padre Felix Varela. Benedict XVI notes: "I am struck by what a remarkably diverse group they are: poor and rich, lay men and women – one a wealthy wife and mother – priests and Sisters, immigrants from afar, the daughter of a Mohawk warrior father and Algonguin mother, another a Haitian slave, and a Cuban intellectual." [511]

The Holy Father concluded with these warm and encouraging remarks which summarized the content of his talk:

> Friends, again I ask you, what about today? What are you seeking? What is God whispering to you? The hope which never disappoints is Jesus Christ. The saints show us the selfless love of his way. As disciples of Christ, their extraordinary journeys unfolded within the community of hope, which is the Church. It is from within the Church that you too will find the courage and support to walk the way of the Lord. Nourished by personal prayer, prompted in silence, shaped by the Church's liturgy you will discover

the particular vocation God has for you. Embrace it with joy. You are Christ's disciples today. Shine his light upon this great city and beyond. Show the world the hope that resonates within you. Tell others about the truth that sets you free. [516]

Another momentous occasion in my priestly life (noted earlier) occurred when I was blessed to concelebrate the Beatification of John Henry Newman in Birmingham, England, on September 19, 2010. Benedict XVI's homily was yet another masterpiece and touchstone of his magisterium on Catholic education. The Pope brilliantly situates Newman in a long line of British saints and scholars, including Saint Bede the Venerable, Saint Hilda, Saint Aelred and Blessed Duns Scotus remarking:

In Blessed John Henry, that tradition of gentle scholarship, deep human wisdom and profound love for the Lord has borne fruit, as a sign of the abiding presence of the Holy Spirit deep within the heart of God's people, bringing forth abundant gifts of holiness." [522]

Arguably, the following paragraph constitutes Benedict XVI's most poignant reflection on Newman as an intellectual and Catholic educator:

> I would like to pay particular tribute to his vision for education, which has done so much to shape the ethos that is the driving force behind Catholic schools and colleges today. Firmly opposed to any reductive or utilitarian approach, he sought to achieve an educational environment in which intellectual training, moral discipline and religious commitment would come together. The project to found a Catholic University in Ireland provided him with an opportunity to develop his ideas on the subject, and the collection of discourses he published as *The Idea of a University* holds up an ideal from which all those engaged in academic formation can continue to learn. And indeed, what better goal could teachers of religion set themselves than Blessed John Henry's famous appeal for an intelligent, well-instructed laity.... [523]

Francis

Jorge Mario Bergoglio, the son of Italian immigrants from Piedmont region in the North, grew up rough and tumble on the mean streets of Buenos Aires with a passion for the Tango and his neighborhood soccer team.

The young Jorge was formed in the typical piety of Catholic Argentina known for its strong Marian devotion and less for its refined theology. His early formation was deeply impacted by his close relationships with his Italian mother and grandmother, whom he frequently mentions, as well as by his icy relationship with his Italian father whom he hardly ever mentions. As a Jesuit scholastic, Jorge not only mastered Latin but grew to love the Byzantine Divine Liturgy which he often volunteered to serve for elderly [retired] Ukrainian Rite Jesuits. As a Jesuit priest, Father Bergoglio exercised authority in an authoritarian yet very efficient way that caused him to rise through the ranks of the Society of Jesus although he was often disliked and resented on account of his rigidity.

For all practical purposes, Bishop Bergoglio was viewed as a theological conservative and admired by

John Paul II for his staunch defense of his landmark Encyclical *Veritatis Splendor*, promulgated in 1993 and later appreciated by Pope Benedict XVI for his work as President of the Episcopal Council of Latin America (CELAM) which, in 2007, produced the beautiful Aparecida document on Christian discipleship and evangelization at the conclusion of its Fifth General Conference.

In 2013, Jorge Mario Bergoglio experienced similar success, as did Joseph Ratzinger in 2005, when many Cardinals expressed enthusiastic approval for his brief pre-conclave homily in which he challenged them to choose a pope who would lead the Church to transcend her boundaries in order to evangelize and interface more effectively with the world and those on the so-called "peripheries" or margins of society – a central theme of his entire pontificate.

As an alumnus of the Pontifical Gregorian University, it strikes me as very odd that the first Jesuit Pope, unlike his modern predecessors, has never bothered to visit the Society of Jesus' premiere University – historically the only school directly founded by Saint Ignatius of Loyola.

It is also peculiar that Pope Francis, a former

high school chemistry and Latin teacher, being that rare Jesuit possessing no graduate degrees, opines very little about Catholic education. With all that having been said, our anthology (pages 534-588) contains several excerpts of Francis on Catholic education. Here are the passages that made the most lasting impression on me:

(1) "[...] by giving youth a sound education, Catholic schools will continue to nourish their human and spiritual formation, in a spirit of dialogue and fraternity with those who do not share their faith. It is important, then, that young Christians receive a high quality catechesis that supports their faith and leads them to an encounter with Christ." [p. 537]

(2) "[...] Catholic schools and universities are attended by many non-Christian students as well as non-believers. Catholic educational institutions offer everyone an education aimed at the integral development of the person that responds to the right of all people to have access to knowledge and understanding. But they are equally called to offer

to all the Christian message – respecting fully the freedom of all and the proper methods of each specific scholastic environment – namely that Jesus Christ is the meaning of life, of the cosmos and of history." [p. 538-539]

(3) "Do not hesitate to enable the greatest number possible of young people to benefit from the proclamation of the Faith, even in public institutions; may the Church be present as well in higher education and in universities, in order to raise awareness of Christian values in those who are responsible for the future of society, so that it may be more human and just." [p.544]

(4) "Never sell off the human and Christian values to which you are witnesses in the family, in schools, and in society. Make your contribution generously so that Catholic schools never become a 'fall-back' solution or an insignificant alternative among the various educational institutions [...] Strive to ensure that Catholic schools are truly open to all! May the Lord Jesus who in the Holy Family of Nazareth increased in stature, in

wisdom and in grace (cf. Lk 2:52) accompany your steps and bless you in your daily commitment." [p. 564]

(5) "With the passing of centuries, schools were established in the neighborhoods of cathedrals and monasteries, thanks especially to the zealous initiatives of bishops and monks. These schools imparted both ecclesiastical doctrine and secular culture, forming them into one whole. From these schools arose the universities, those glorious institutions of the Middle Ages which, from their beginning, had the Church as their most bountiful mother and patroness." [p. 568]

(6) "With the intention of providing concrete responses to the requests of his time in the education field, John Baptist de La Salle undertook bold forms of teaching methods. In this respect, he was moved by an extraordinary pedagogical realism. He substituted the French language for Latin, which had normally been used in teaching; he separated the students into homogenous learning groups in view of more effective work; he established seminaries for countryside teach-

ers, that is for young people who wanted to become teachers without becoming part of any religious institution; he founded Sunday schools for adults and two hostels, one for juvenile delinquents and another for the rehabilitation of the incarcerated. He dreamt of a school open to everyone; for this reason he did not hesitate to address even extreme educational necessities, by introducing a method of rehabilitation through school and work. In these formative realities he initiated a corrective pedagogy which, in contrast to the customs of the times, brought study and work to young people under sentence – with arts and crafts rather than just a cell or lashes." [pages 583-584]

Conclusion

As George Weigel elucidates in his book, *The Irony of Modern Church History: How the Church Rediscovered & Challenged the Modern World to Reform*, and likewise Professor Owen E. Cummings in his ambitious tome, *Popes, Councils and Theology: From Pope Pius IX to Pope Francis*, the modern Popes never miss an opportunity to be educators and teachers of the Catholic Faith and social doctrine, not to mention Vatican diplomacy in diverse and complicated circumstances whose surface we have only scratched in this presentation.

Time and again, as our anthology relates on every page, the modern Popes addressed Catholic administrators, educators, and students about the inestimable value of a Catholic education. They did not address this topic in a vacuum, but instead tailored it to specific audiences, young and old alike, and in so doing were capable in a remarkable fashion of underscoring the uniqueness of Catholic education, as well as its marvelous integration into every aspect of the human person's individual and communal development.

It is clear that the modern Popes regard Catholic

education not as some peripheral reality but rather as one essential to Catholic identity and mission and indeed as the logical extension of the family as the "domestic church."

In particular, they emphasize that, as the Catholic school goes, so goes the Church. They perceived, each in his own way, that Catholic education is where the Church's beloved children find a sure and certain home for their hearts, minds, and spirits as they mature in wisdom, age, and grace before God and man.

From the perspective of the authentic papal magisterium over the course of the past century, the Catholic school is a privileged instrument of saving grace in human society and an indispensable element of the Church's life – inexorably linked to every facet of her doctrine and devotion.

The modern Popes stressed, to varying degrees and with different pedagogical styles and magisterial methods, how Catholic education interacts with and sheds light on every sector of intellectual endeavor and how, in plumbing the depths of an authentic Catholic education, we discover its nexus to the Church's inestimable cultural and artistic patrimony and even more fundamentally to the integral beauty, goodness and truth of her Creed, Code, and Cult.

Finally, I would like to express my heartfelt hope that my doctoral work will constitute in the words of Father Stravinskas, "a major contribution to the documentation of the Holy See related to Catholic education, providing invaluable resources to bishops, superintendents of diocesan school systems, pastors, principals, and parents involved in diocesan or parish school boards."

Many thanks for your gracious attention and Godspeed in your deliberations!

www.ingramcontent.com/pod-product-compliance
Lightning Source LLC
Chambersburg PA
CBHW060847050426
42453CB00008B/878